A Love Letter to Cinema

By

A crazy artist with an imagination named

Joel Brown

A LOVE LETTER TO CINEMA

Copyright © 2017 Joel Brown

All rights reserved.

ISBN-10: 1982041161
ISBN-13: 978-1982041168

DEDICATION

First and Foremost to God-Jesus Christ, my Mother-Sheila Brown, and the Paramount Theater; nevertheless to all the others and the Second-Run Theaters - "The movie theatre has been a much-needed refuge during times of trouble... During the Depression, viewers were swept away by the sunny-natured Shirley Temple, making them forget about their troubles for a while. It was farewell to all the worries and cares of the day. When the Paramount Theater opened its doors, we forgot about names like Hitler and Mussolini. It was time instead to unwind and dream a little. The Paramount introduced new young singers like Frank Sinatra, and showed films with big stars like Clark Gable and Betty Hutton. These were the times that tried men's souls, but the glitz and glamour of Hollywood kept us distracted and entertained. We retained our perspective, and most importantly, allowed ourselves to hold on, to our national sense of humor."

Ezekiel 25:17 "The path of the righteous man I beset on all side by the inequities of the selfish and the tyranny of evil men. Blessed is he who, in the name of charity and good will, shepherds the weak through the valley of the darkness. For he is truly his brother's keeper and the finder of lost children. And I will strike down with great vengeance and furious anger those who attempt to poison and destroy my brothers. And you will know I am the Lord when I lay my vengeance upon you."

CONTENTS

	Acknowledgments	i
1	Newspaper	Pg 0-1
2	Early-Birds	Pg 2-3
3	Ticket Stub	Pg 4-5
4	Concessions	Pg 6-7
5	Movie Searcher	Pg 8-9
6	Na-cho Movie	Pg 10-11
7	Movie Magic Community	Pg 12-13
8	Those Movie Reactions	Pg 14-15
9	Down with the Credits	Pg 16-17
10	24-hours in a Movie Theater	Pg 18-19
11	Movie Fandom	Pg 20-21
12	The Cry for Authenticity	Pg 22-23

ACKNOWLEDGMENTS

"The Lord is my director; I have no objective or no need to use the Stanislavsky method or Meisner technique. He makes me to recline back in cozy theaters; He shows me pleasant motion pictures. He blows my mind; He sends me on a journey of adventure for all His glory. Yaaas, though I'm blocked through scenes of horrible darkness, I'll fear no evil; for You make a cameo with me and steal the show; Your props and Your set, they comfort me. You provide a crafts service for me 24/7 in front of my critics; You capture my best headshot with grace and no Photoshop; my thirst is quenched, because there is unlimited refills. Expecting popcorn, raisin nets, sprite (goodness), discounts and bonuses (mercy) to follow me. Throughout the movie showings of my life; and I will rest with my eyes open in the theater of my director for all eternity."

— Joel Brown's personal version of Psalm 23

THE NEWSPAPER

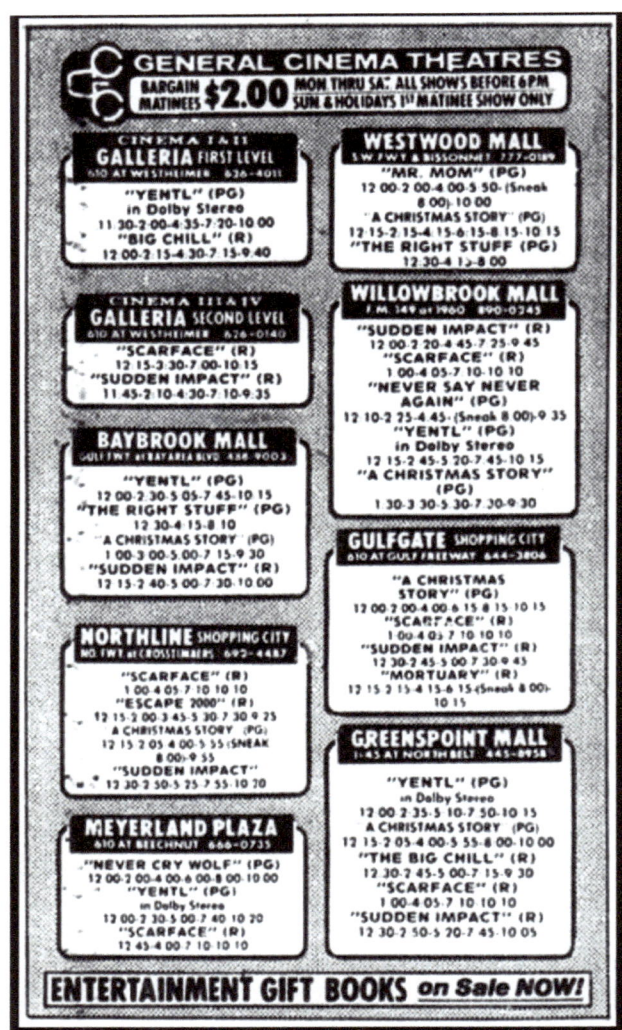

It's priceless when...

...you get to get in the car to drive to the gas station or local grocery store to pick up a local newspaper, just to get the show times to go watch a second-run movie.

Now that's authenticity.

THE EARLY-BIRDS GETS TO ROAM OR WAIT

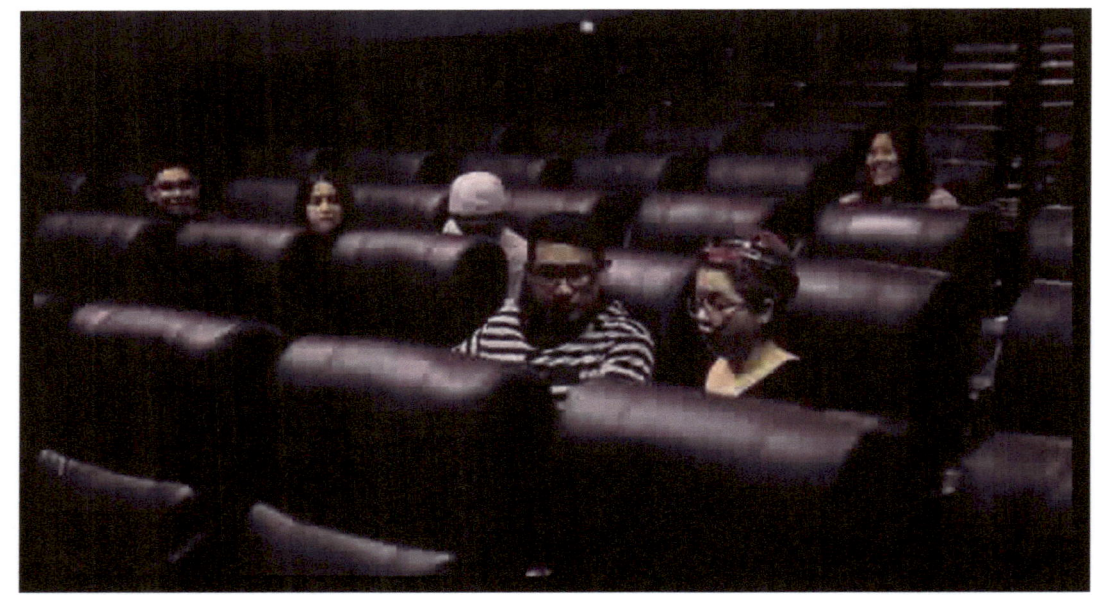

It's priceless when...

...you get dressed in style to go to a movie and leave out early; not just so you can keep yourself from walking in late, but also so you can catch the previews. However, this leaves you winding up going off into the mall to wander around for a bit as spur-of-the-moment plan for doing something in waits for the time of a movie showing to draw near; due to getting there too early.

Now that's authenticity.

THE TICKET STUB

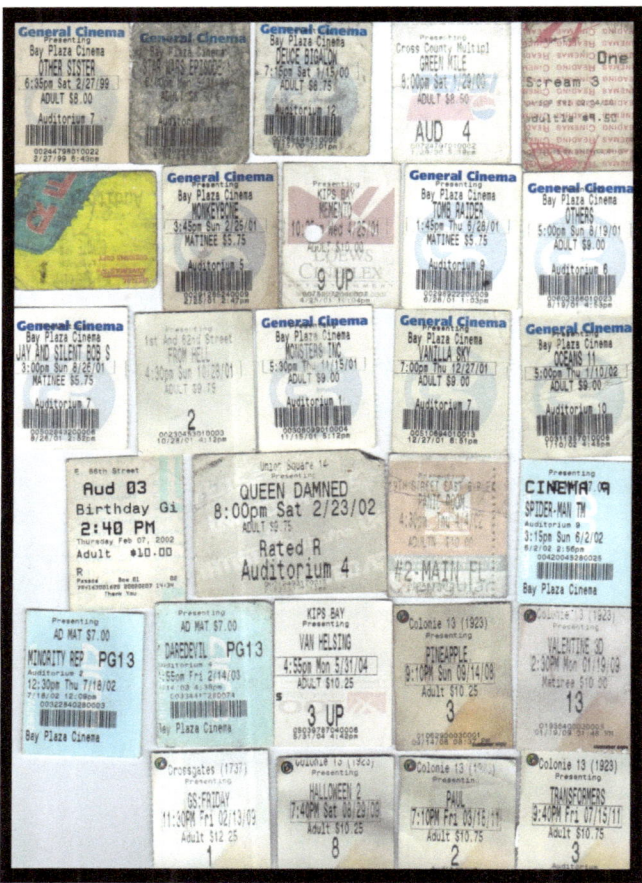

It's priceless when...

...you go to the box office to get that tiny, piece of paper for the cost of a $10 matinee movie that allows you access to the movie beyond the ticket booth, in which one half gets torn off and the other half winds up being kept as a souvenir; just so you can remember all that has happened in your experience of this movie. Ahh, movie moments.

Now that's authenticity.

CONCESSIONS

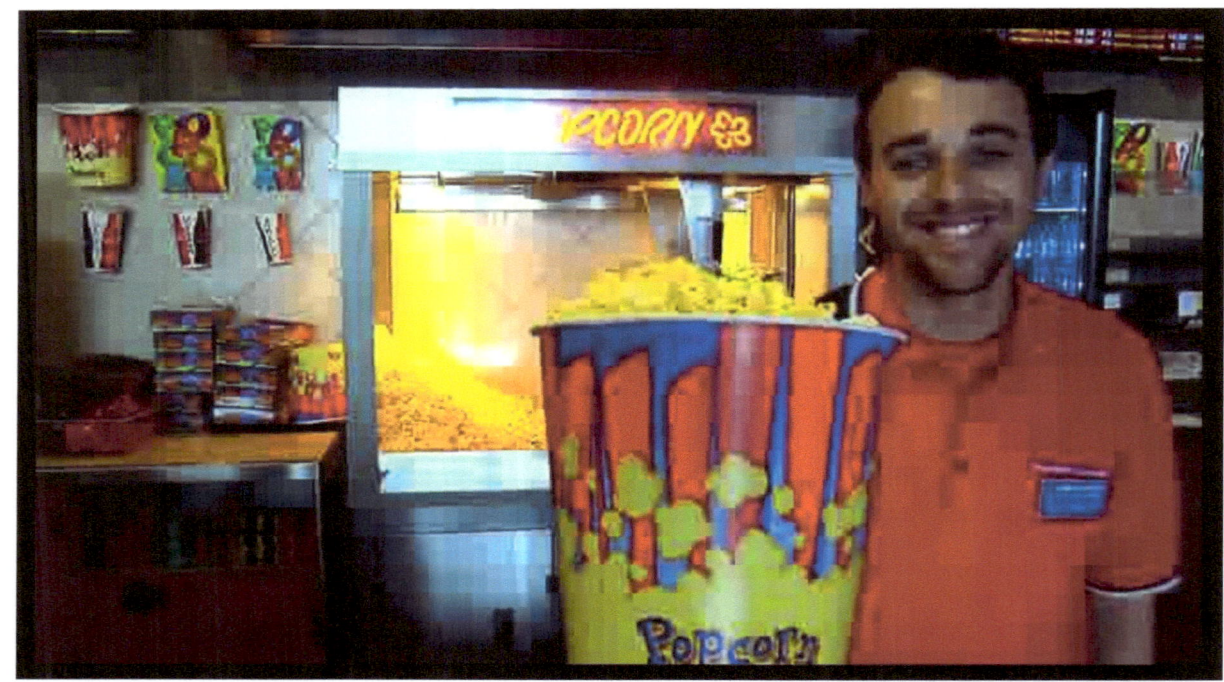

It's priceless when...

...you go to the concession stand to get the basic necessities which are: a medium buttered popcorn, medium sprite or Dr. Pepper, Raisinets, and cherry licorice; just so you can be doing something besides just sitting there while you are watching the movie. Only to upsize it to a large popcorn and drink, as you know you won't be finishing it and will probably be either taking it home or leaving it in the seat.

Now that's authenticity.

MOVIE SEARCHER

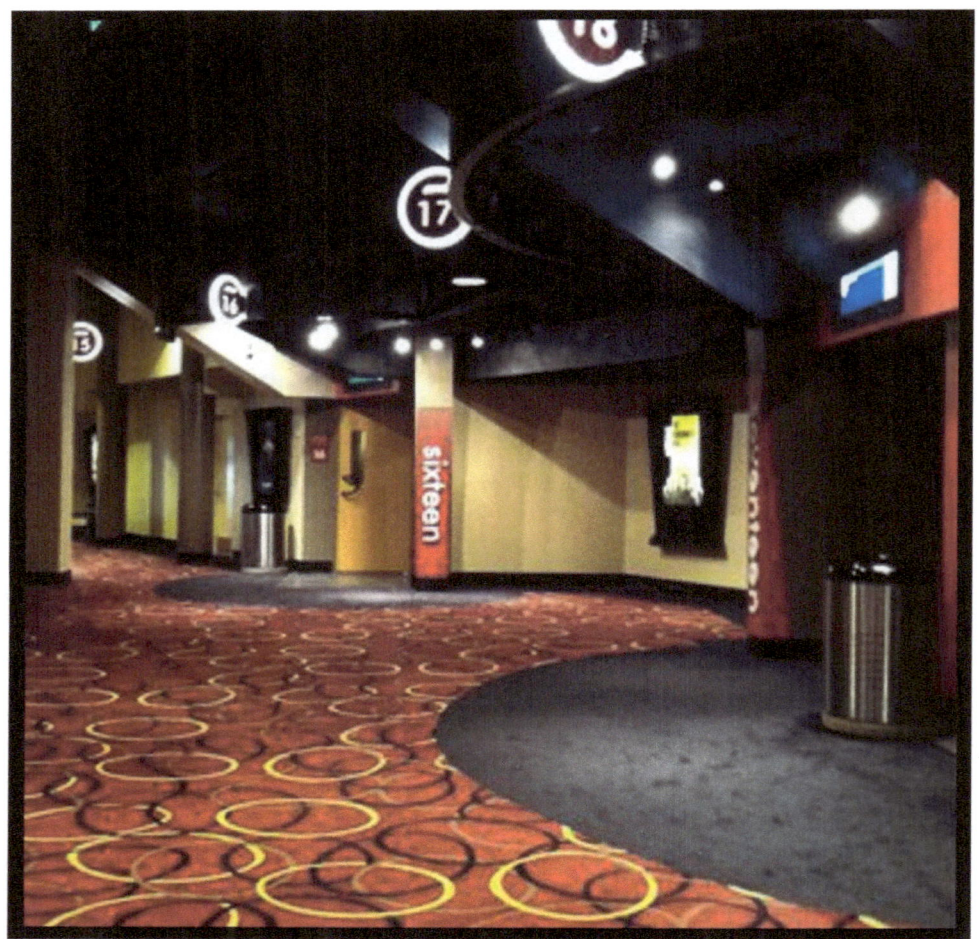

It's priceless when...

...you're looking for the movie down one hallway and have to turn around after you have figured out that it's probably on the opposite side; with the numbers above the theater door reading, even down one hall and odd down another.

Now that's authenticity

NA-CHO MOVIE YOU PAID TO SEE

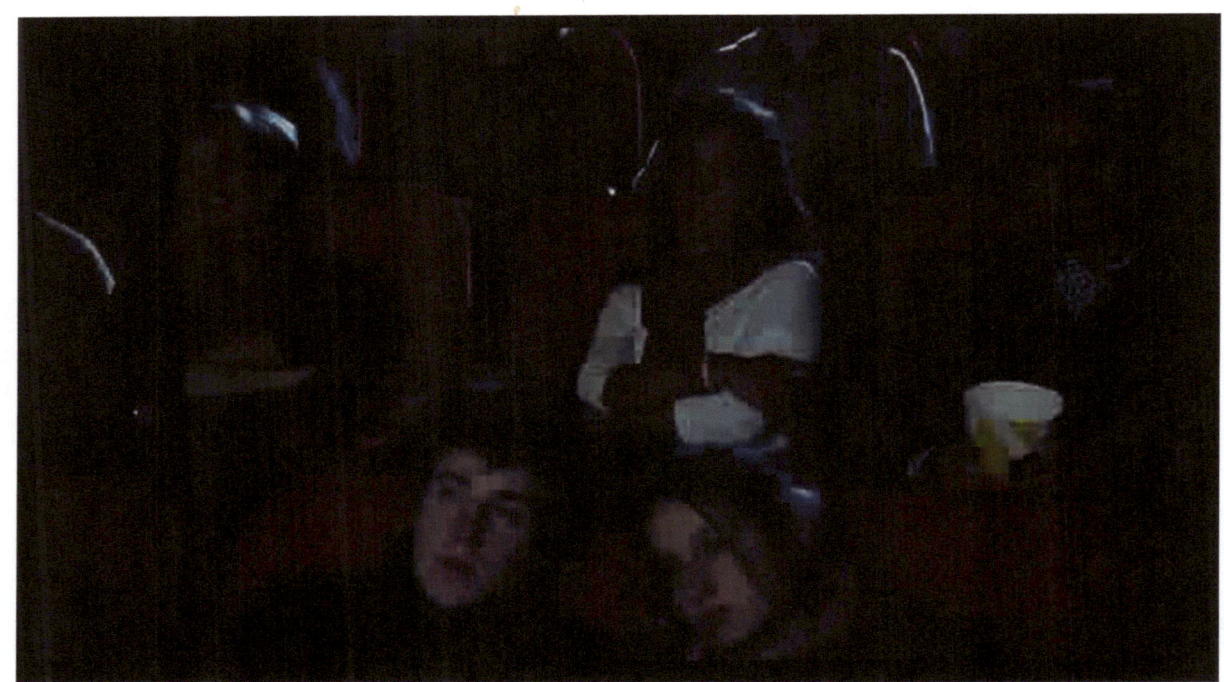

It's priceless when...

...you find the theater room that looks like it's showing the movie that you have paid to see, but as you get as far as going inside and even finding a good seat that makes you feel comfy, after you have been sitting through all of the previews up unto the start of the movie; you find out that it's not the movie you were supposed to be seeing. Unless, that is, you're a movie hopper. Otherwise, you quietly get up with slight embarrassment to walk out of the theater to go find the right movie that you paid to see.

Now that's authenticity.

IN A COMMUNITY WITH MOVIE MAGIC

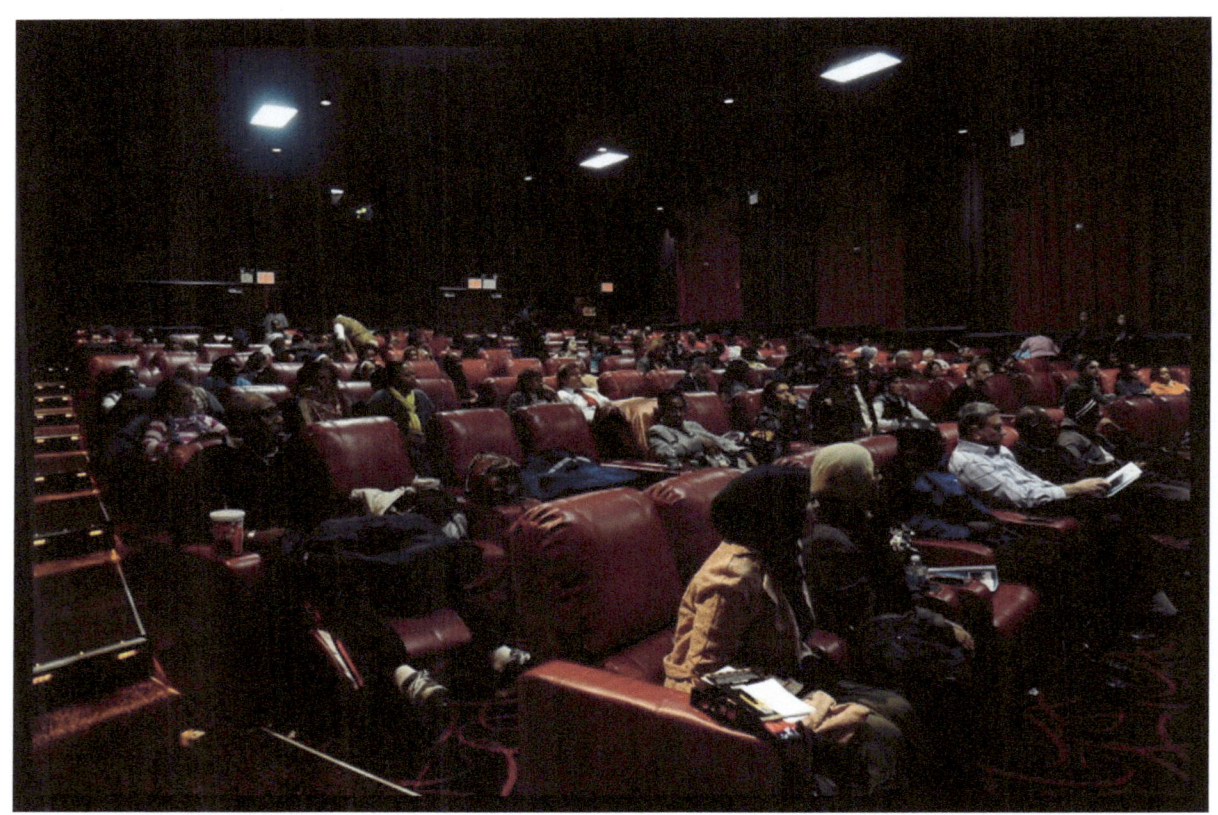

It's priceless when...

...you're in the right movie theater and by luck that it hasn't started, but a few minutes into the previews. You got you refreshments all in the right places: drink in the right cup holder, candies in the left cup holder, and a popcorn bag between your legs. You smell a fresh aroma of popcorn that mixes in with a scent of smuggled in chicken or some kind of outside food, as you hear people talking under their breath with cellphone sounds going off in the midst of glowing pools of light that spills out on to their faces. While you lean back in your seat, putting your feet on the top of the seat that is in front of you; being careful not to let the person know it or brush a foot up against their head to cause a disruption. As the movie starts, silence becomes golden as all screens go black and suddenly. Our devotion is fixed on a silver screen that's on the wall before us as a photoplay is projected with captivating illusions that's on display, pulling us into the story as the audience becomes one; like a story being told to kids around a campfire.

Now that's authenticity.

MOVIE REACTIONS

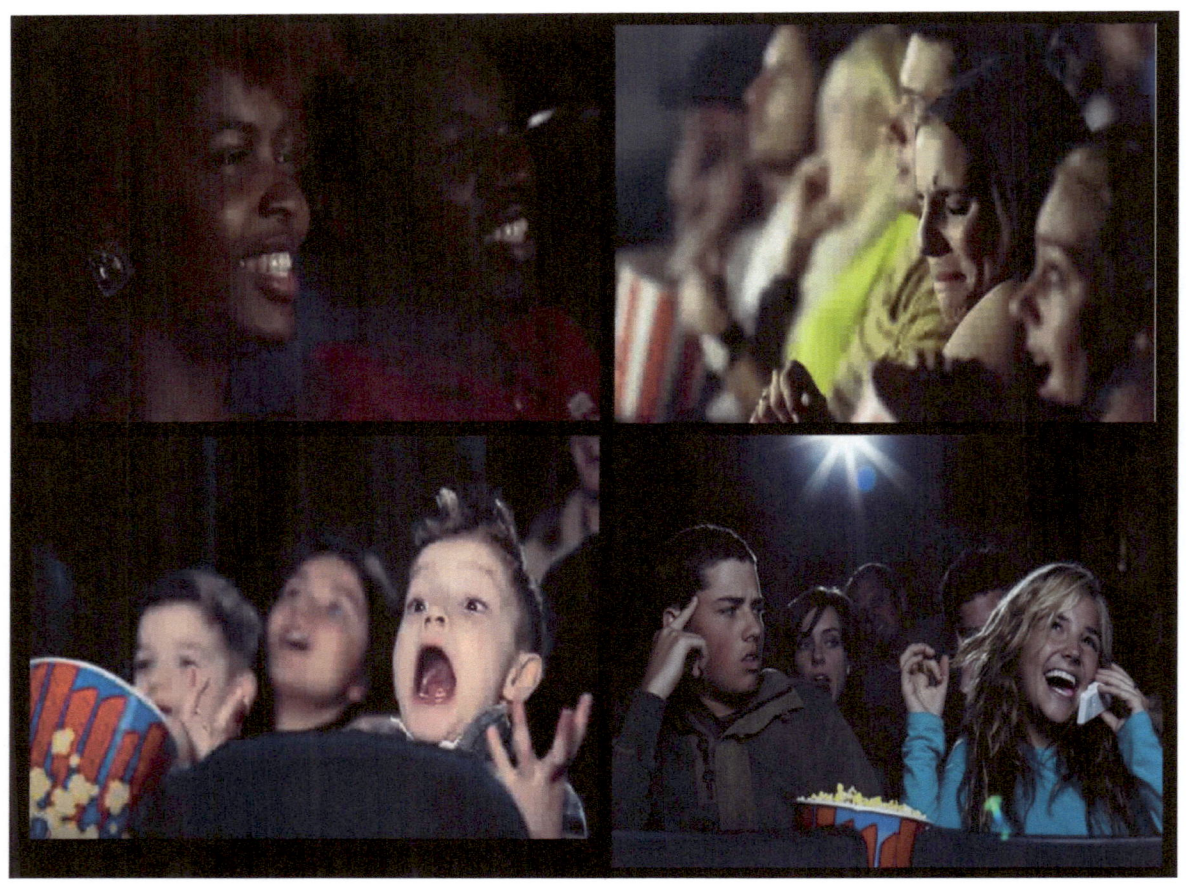

It's priceless when...

...seeing people's reaction to the movie – like the jumps, screams, laughs, and of course the talkbacks – during the movie; it makes you grateful that you can have a share in this common interest with complete strangers that just so happen to be in community with you in a movie theater.

Now that's authenticity.

GOING DOWN WITH THE END CREDITS

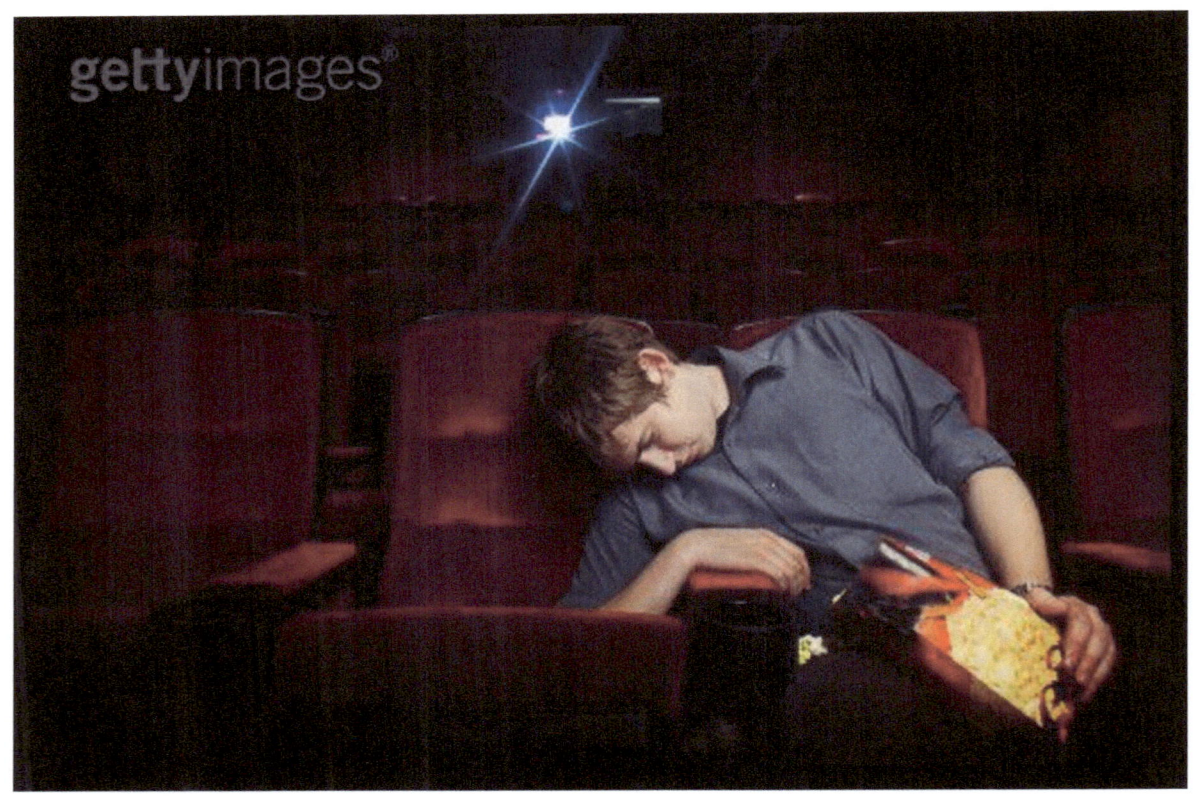

It's priceless when...

After the movie, you find yourself staying till the very last words of the credits as you notice your surroundings; seems all too strange. Like the heads of people look like they have shrunk under the dimmed lighting, as if, all the knowledge that was in their head had been pulled out of it and went straight into the film projector. Another thing that might seem a bit strange is shoes left behind, popcorn spread all around the floor, and finding a person asleep towards the middle or front row in the theater. You stand in awe of the funny and strange things that can be discovered in a movie theater, making you curiously ponder up your own stories for its reason of being; these movie participates have now left behind stories of their own for the ushers to collect that are brought to security as souvenirs.

Now that's authenticity.

24-HOURS IN A MOVIE THEATER

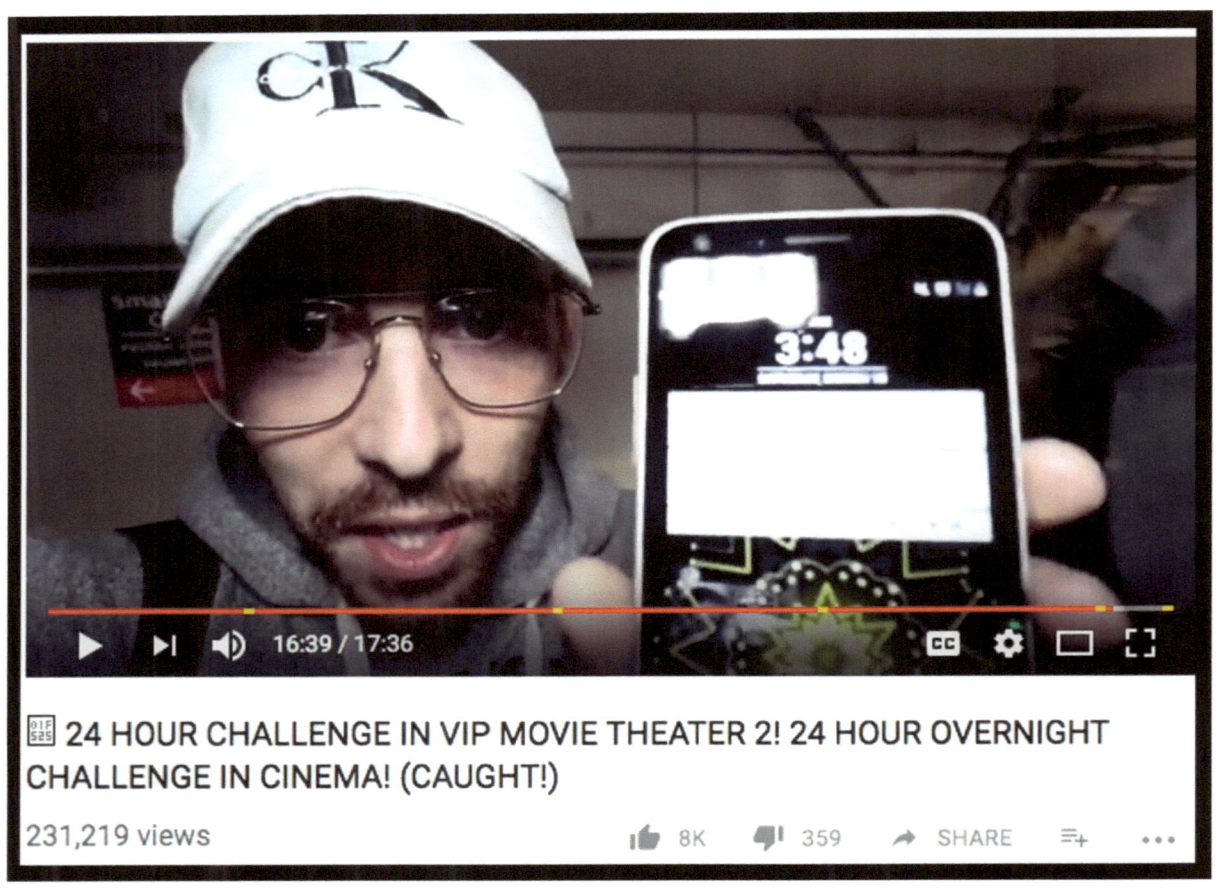

It's priceless when...

...you don't want to leave the movie theater as you have got caught up in that whole world with insights, flooding your mind from what the movie has taught you. Until you friends inject you with an idea of staying 24-hours in a movie theater and daring you to rise to the challenge; just to try to make a YouTube video that will go viral, but someone always does something stupid to get everyone caught.

Now that's authenticity.

YOUR FLIX FRIENDS: PARASOCIAL RELATIONSHIPS THROUGH FLIX

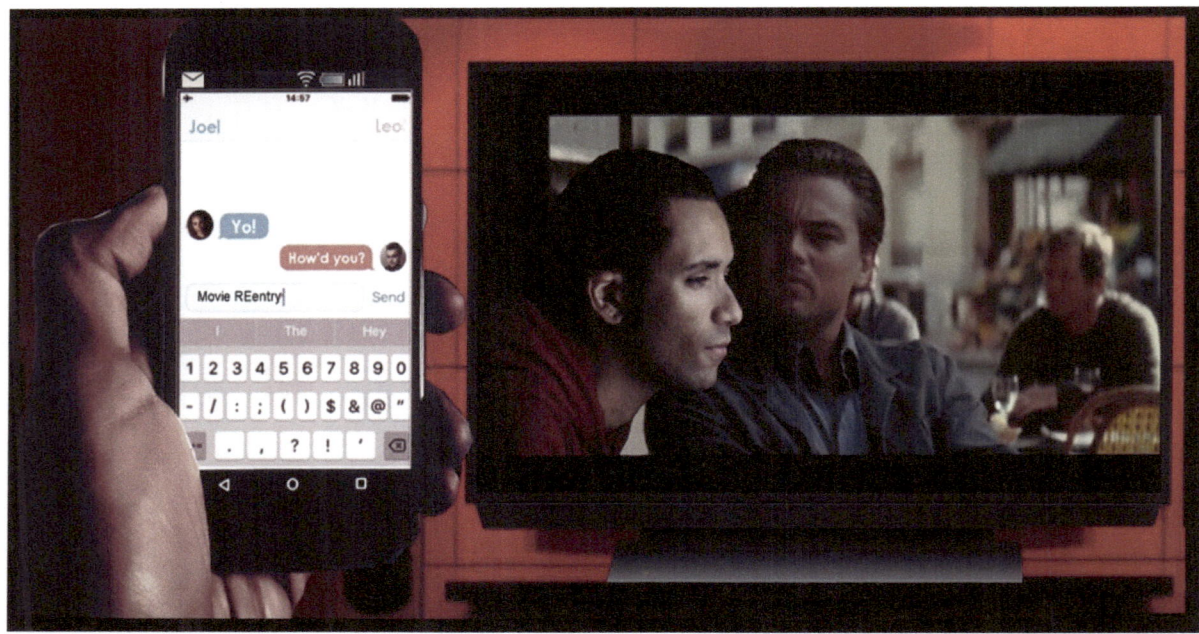

It's priceless when...

...you get in your car, putting the ticket stub; either in your wallet or ash tray and just before driving off. You look up the movie on IMDb.com that you have just seen and get "the skinny" on your favorite actor who played the character that you related most with as your parasocial relationship has just begun and takes its own turn into fandom from there.

Now that's authenticity.

A HEART-RENDERING CRY FOR AUTHENTICITY

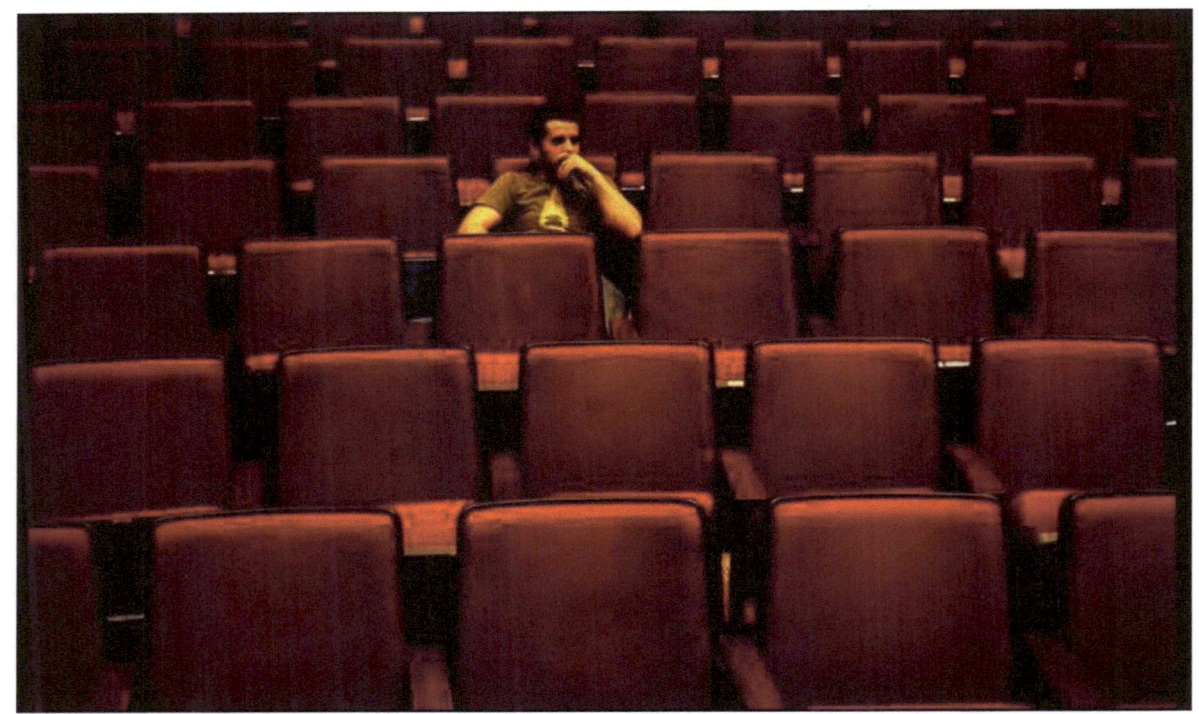

It's priceless now...

...with movies being streamed online, everything is on-demand as we have gave up a lot; just to have everything that we ever wanted at our fingertips for instant gratification. Where all you have to do is go to your TV or computer, and browse a catalogue that houses a list of movie showings after they have been released from the theater; just to be able to watch it in the comfort of our own homes.

With that in mind...

Could we have reached a heart-rendering cry for authenticity?

As technology enhances, it costs us something that was authentic that seems to replace it - like the movie theaters crossing over from film projectors to digital projectors that will leave many projectionists without a job.

Yet this is why I love collecting DVDs of movies because it's more like a souvenir, holding a memory of an experience that you had when you first saw a particular movie at the cinema; nevertheless, it's a symbol of authenticity that you get as an add-on when you go to purchase a movie that you can't get with a digital purchase. Thus, a DVD is like a time capsule that give you something to point on a shelf when you're an old man, telling stories of authenticity of how things use to be with movies as you share with your grand kids - who probably will be in an age of virtual, holographic movies.

ACCOLADE

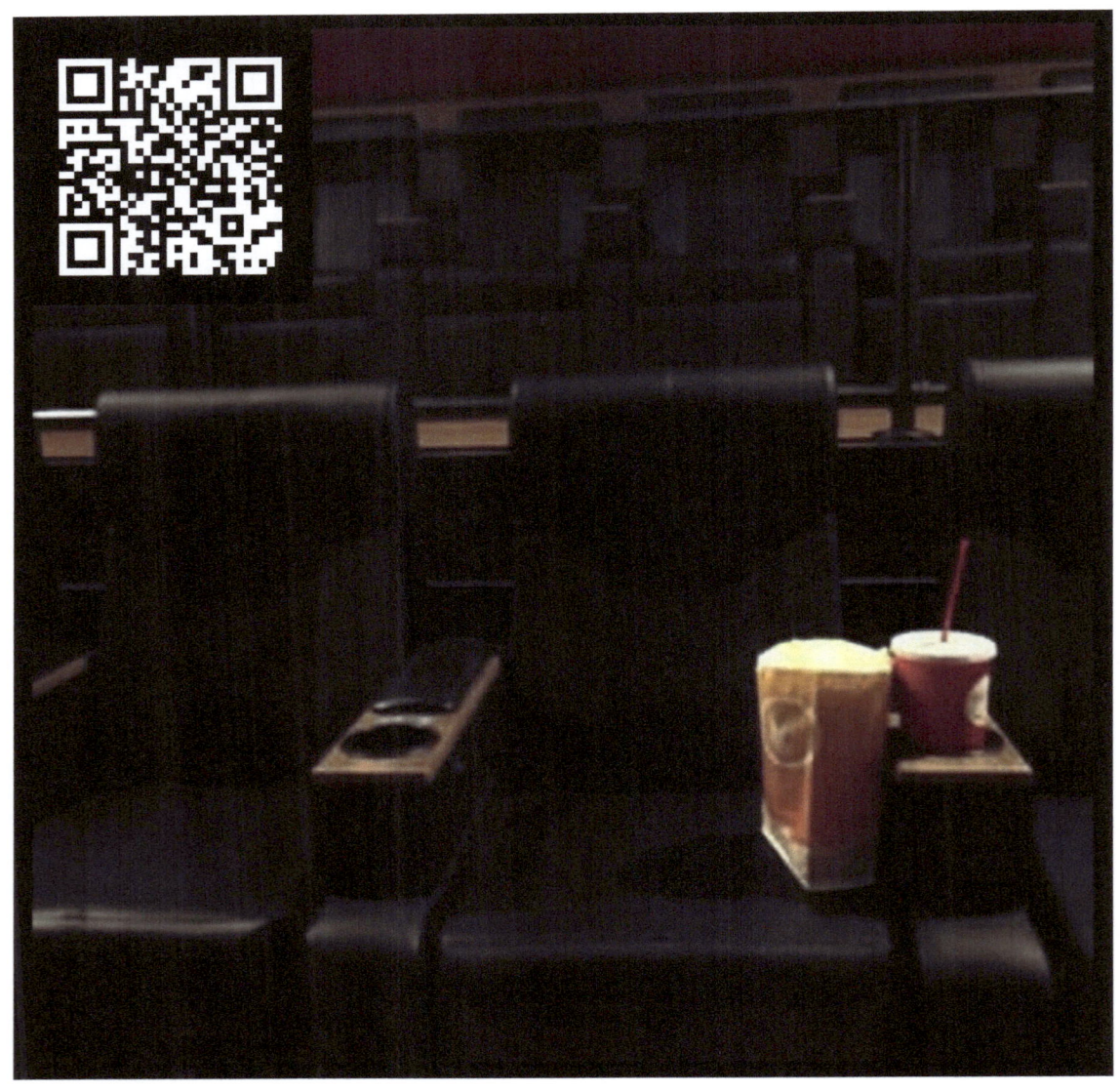

ABOUT THE ARTISTIC AUTHOR

   Once upon a time there was a mysterious boy with a dream he carried in his heart that came with uncommon gifts and unique talents, who finds creative ways to adjust to his present limitations. Everyday the boy would do his best in using what he had to make something out of what he had, even if it was in the midst of having nothing. One day hard times hit, yet out of it brought forth an invention and from his oppression came creativity –The Imagineer Writer – scripting those things that be not as though they were. Because of that, a rediscovery happened that caused opposing things work for the boy. Until finally, the boy dawned upon a revelation that led him to writing this motto that he begun to live out: "Life is what you make it, so make it like a movie and act your best." Thus, the boy continued to nurture what's best about himself and became stronger through his love for the theater arts. So the boy grew into an artist, who had this gift of writing. Every day he'd practice creative imagination, who finds that he hates seeing people abandoned in insurmountable situations that left them with suicide being the only option due to having had experienced this himself. One day, in a theatrical scene design course he made a diorama. Because of that, an idea embarked upon him to start crafting character dioramas that memorializes the stars who died in an insurmountable situation by suicide. Because of that, he wants to raise awareness and build a support system. Until finally this divine discontent gave him the vision to create a company from the growing up.

Now you enter the story by completing the ad-libs:

   Eventually, _____ (your name) crossed paths with him via _____ (Noun-person, place or thing) ; who became like a parasocial friend to the artist and there was a _____ (Animal) named _____ (Color) that _____ (Verb-action word), everyday Joel and _____ (your name) would use their _____ (Body part-single) to develop _____ (character strength) with the _____ (Animal) for _____ (Person) one day who's in a _____ (silly word) predicament because of that, they _____ (Verb-action word) together. Until finally, _____ (silly word).

FINAL THOUGHTS FROM THE ARTISTIC AUTHOR

Through my own experiences with cinema I've discovered how cinema is a gift that unwraps movies; to bless with a screen flickering story, surround sound seat shaking experience where child-like belief inspires us to creative miracles of healing and growth. Cinema is such a sacred place as it's the only place where guards come down and defenses drop; to form trust, letting a message drive straight into the heart that speaks to one in their own language. Movies have a way of taking us in and out of a dark place that life and mentors us through our state-of-being, when there's no one to go to for mentorship. Movies have a way of taking us in and out of the dark place that life has us in, as it mentors us through our state-of-being - it's a quiet place where one can find peace away from the storms of life. A movie provides a role-model from the movie screen through our favorite actor that allows one to be parented, offering guidance that teaches with the character's life. While gaining a positive perspective with an alternative ending from a reel-to-real life, inspiring character strengths and virtues within us. Cinema is a place to practice creative imagination, as it's like a pasture of entertainment and river of education. So thanks to all the movie theaters for creating a place of refuge for the people.

WORKS CITED

movieglu.files.wordpress.com/2014/06/newspaper-listings2-1983

Getty Images

photos.cinematreasures.org

cinematreatures.org

'Movie Theaters: How To Optimize Your Experience' by groupon.com via Youtube

'24 HOUR CHALLENGE IN VIP MOVIE THEATER 2 ! 24 HOUR OVERNIGHT CHALLENGE IN CINEMA! (CAUGHT!)' by ImJayStation via YouTube.com

www.ingramcontent.com/pod-product-compliance
Lightning Source LLC
Chambersburg PA
CBHW040453220526
45473CB00004B/1620